# TOUCHSTONE

## WORKBOOK 1A

MICHAEL MCCARTHY

JEANNE MCCARTEN

HELEN SANDIFORD

CAMBRIDGE
UNIVERSITY PRESS

Shaftesbury Road, Cambridge CB2 8EA, United Kingdom

One Liberty Plaza, 20th Floor, New York, NY 10006, USA

477 Williamstown Road, Port Melbourne, VIC 3207, Australia

314–321, 3rd Floor, Plot 3, Splendor Forum, Jasola District Centre, New Delhi – 110025, India

103 Penang Road, #05–06/07, Visioncrest Commercial, Singapore 238467

Cambridge University Press & Assessment is a department of the University of Cambridge.

We share the University's mission to contribute to society through the pursuit of education, learning and research at the highest international levels of excellence.

www.cambridge.org
Information on this title: www.cambridge.org/9781107670716

First published 2005
Second edition 2014

20  19  18  17  16  15  14  13  12  11  10  9  8  7  6  5

Printed in Great Britain by Ashford Colour Press Ltd.

*A catalogue record for this publication is available from the British Library*

ISBN  978-1-107-67987-0 Student's Book
ISBN  978-1-107-62792-5 Student's Book A
ISBN  978-1-107-65345-0 Student's Book B
ISBN  978-1-107-63933-1 Workbook
ISBN  978-1-107-67071-6 Workbook A
ISBN  978-1-107-69125-4 Workbook B
ISBN  978-1-107-68330-3 Full Contact
ISBN  978-1-107-66769-3 Full Contact A
ISBN  978-1-107-61366-9 Full Contact B
ISBN  978-1-107-64223-2 Teacher's Edition with Assessment Audio CD/CD-ROM
ISBN  978-1-107-61414-7 Class Audio CDs (4)

Additional resources for this publication at www.cambridge.org/touchstone2

# Contents

# All about you

## Lesson A — Hello and good-bye

### 1 Meetings and greetings

Vocabulary | **A** Complete the conversations. Choose and write the best response.

1. A Hello.

   B *Hi.*

   (a.) Hi.

   b. Good-bye.

2. A Hi. I'm Ted.

   B _____

   a. Hi, I'm Lucille. Nice to meet you.

   b. See you next week.

3. A How are you?

   B _____

   a. I'm Kyle.

   b. I'm fine, thanks.

4. A Good-bye.

   B _____

   a. See you later.

   b. Thanks.

5. A Good night.

   B _____

   a. Hello.

   b. Bye. See you tomorrow.

6. A Hi. How are you?

   B _____

   a. Good, thanks. How are you?

   b. Have a nice day.

Vocabulary **B** **Complete the conversations with the expressions in the box.**

| | | | |
|---|---|---|---|
| Good night. | ✓Hello. | How are you? | Nice to meet you. |
| Have a good evening. | Hi. | I'm fine | See you |

1. Jack ___Hello.___ I'm Jack.

   Anna _____ I'm Anna.

   Jack _____

2. Sonia Hi, Julie. How are you?

   Julie Good. _____

   Sonia _____ , thanks.

3. Mike _____

   Koji Thanks. You too.

4. Joan _____

   Mary Bye. _____ tomorrow.

**C** **Complete the instant message.**

| Instant Message ⬛🗗✕ |
|---|
| Sandra Good morning, Jenny. |
| Jenny ___Good morning___ , Sandra. |
| Sandra _____ are you? |
| Jenny _____ , thanks. _____ |
| Sandra Good. |
| Jenny See you later. |
| Sandra OK. _____ a nice day. |
| Jenny Thanks. _____ too. |
| Sandra Bye. |

### 1 My name's Eva.

Vocabulary Complete the conversation.

A   Good morning.

B   Good morning.

A   How are you?

B   I'm fine.

A   What's your __name__?

B   Eva Salazar.

A   How do you spell your _____ name?

B   It's S-A-L-A-Z-A-R.

A   And what's your _____ name?

B   Eva.

A   OK. How do you _____ *Eva*?

B   E-V-A.

A   And are you Ms., Miss, or _____ ?

B   Ms.

A   Thank you. Have a nice day.

B   Thanks. You too.

### 2 Your personal information

Vocabulary Complete the form. Use your own information.

## *Touchstone* English Club

NAME: _____

       First           Middle           Last

☐ single    ☐ married

CLASS: _____

ROOM: _____

TEACHER: _____

# 3 Are we in the same class?

Grammar **A** Complete the conversation. Write *am* or *are*. Use contractions *'m* or *'re* where possible.

Receptionist   Hello. ___*Are*___ you here for
an English class?

Mi-Young   Yes, I _____ . I'm Mi-Young.

Receptionist   Mi-Young Lee? You _____ in Class C.

Mi-Young   Thank you.

Sergio   Hi. _____ I in Class C, too? I'm Sergio.

Receptionist   Yes, you _____ .

Sergio   So we _____ in the same class.

Receptionist   Wait. _____ you Sergio Rodrigues?

Sergio   No, I _____ not. I'm Sergio Lopes.

Receptionist   Oh, you _____ in Class D.
You _____ not in the same class.

**B** Complete the conversation.

David   Hi. _____ _____ Julia Kim?

Leti   No, _____ _____ . I'm Leticia Martinez,
but everyone calls me Leti.

David   Hi, Leti. I'm David. Nice to meet you.

Leti   _____ _____ here for a dance class?

David   Yes, _____ _____ . _____ _____
in the same class?

Leti   Yes, _____ _____ . We're in Class A.

# 4 About you

Grammar **Answer the questions. Use your own information.**

1.  Are you in an English class?

   _____

2.  Are you in a French class?

   _____

3.  How are you today?

   _____

4.  Are you and your friends in the same English class?

   _____

5.  Are you married?

   _____

### 1 What's the number?

Vocabulary **A** Write the numbers.

| 0 | 1 | 2 | 3 | 4 | 5 |
|---|---|---|---|---|---|
| zero | _____ | _____ | _____ | _____ | _____ |

| 6 | 7 | 8 | 9 | 10 |
|---|---|---|---|---|
| _____ | _____ | _____ | _____ | _____ |

**B** Complete the crossword puzzle.

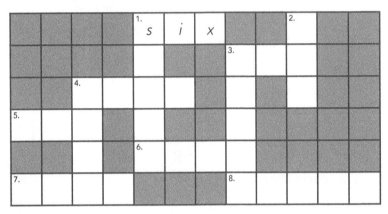

**Across**

1. two × three = ___six___

3. two + eight = _____

4. ten ÷ two = _____

5. six – four = _____

6. three + six = _____

7. five × zero = _____

8. six + two = _____

**Down**

1. ten – three = _____

2. eight – seven = _____

3. eight – five = _____

4. two × two = _____

### 2 What's the word?

Vocabulary The letters spell a word. Write each letter in the correct box below to see the word.

| 1. C | 3. H | 5. N | 7. E | 9. U |
|------|------|------|------|------|
| 2. O | 4. O | 6. T | 8. S | 10. T |

| ten | four | nine | one | three | eight | six | two | five | seven |
|-----|------|------|-----|-------|-------|-----|-----|------|-------|
|     |      |      | C   |       |       |     |     |      |       |

## 3 Here's your membership card.

**Grammar** Look at Mark's student ID card. Write his answers in the conversation.

Lee Hello. Are you a member of the club?

Mark No, I'm not.

Lee OK. Well, here's an application form.
So, what's your last name?

Mark _It's Brokaw._ **or** _Brokaw._
**or** _My last name's Brokaw._

Lee Thank you. And your first name?

Mark _____

Lee What's your middle initial, please?

Mark _____

Lee And what's your email address?

Mark _____

Lee And your phone number?

Mark _____

Lee Are you an English student?

Mark _____

Lee What's your teacher's name?

Mark _____

Lee Thank you. Here's your membership card.
Have a nice day.

Student ID Card
Mark A. Brokaw

Telephone: 740-555-2968
Email: mab@cup.org
Department: English (Mrs. Roberts)

## 4 About you

**Grammar and vocabulary** Write questions with *What's* and the words given. Then answer the questions
with your own information.

1. A _What's your name?_
      (your name)

   B _____

2. A _____
      (your cell phone number)

   B _____

3. A _____
      (your email address)

   B _____

4. A _____
      (your English teacher's name)

   B _____

## 1 Good evening.

Conversation strategies | **Complete the conversations with the expressions in the box. Use each expression only one time.**

| | | | | | |
|---|---|---|---|---|---|
| Good evening. | ✓ Hi | How about you? | How are you doing? | Thank you. | Yes |
| Pretty good. | Hello. | Nice to meet you. | Good-bye. | thanks. | Yeah |

1. Sam    Hi, Ali.

   Ali    ____*Hi*____ , Sam. _____

   Sam    Good, thanks. How about you?

   Ali    _____

   Sam    Am I late?

   Ali    _____ , you are, but it's OK.

   Sam    Good. By the way, here's your book.

   Ali    Oh, _____

2.  Joe    Good evening.

    Clerk    _____ What's your name, please?

    Joe    Joe Johnson.

    Clerk    Oh, yes. Mr. Johnson. Your room number is

    10A. Here's your key.

    Joe    _____

3. Sally    Hello. My name's Sally.

   Kate    _____ I'm Kate. _____

   Are you here on business?

   Sally    _____ , I am. _____

   Kate    No, I'm on vacation.

   Sally    Nice. Oh, here's a taxi. _____

   Kate    Bye.

## 2 How are you doing?

Conversation strategies **A** Rewrite the conversation. Use less formal expressions for the underlined words.

A <u>Hello. How are you?</u>    A *Hi. How are you doing?*

B <u>I'm fine, thank you.</u> How are you?    B _____

A <u>I'm fine.</u> Are you a student here?    A _____

B <u>Yes,</u> I am. How about you?    B _____

A <u>Yes,</u> me too.    A _____

B What's the email address here?

A It's goodschool1@cup.org.

B <u>Thank you. Good-bye.</u>    B _____

A <u>Good-bye.</u>    A _____

**B** Number the lines of the conversation in the correct order. Then write the conversation.

___ Hi.    A *Hello.*

___ Yeah, me too.    B _____

___ OK.    A _____

___ Are you here for the concert?    B _____

___ How are you doing?    A _____

_1_ Hello.    B _____

___ Yeah, I am. How about you?    A _____

## Unit 1 Progress chart

| What can you do? Mark the boxes. ✓ = I can . . .   ? = I need to review how to . . . | To review, go back to these pages in the Student's Book. |
|---|---|
| **Grammar** | |
| ☐ make statements with *I'm (not)*, *you're (not)*, and *we're (not)*. | 2, 4, and 5 |
| ☐ ask questions with *Are you . . . ?* | 5 |
| ☐ ask questions with *What's . . . ?* | 4, 6, and 7 |
| ☐ give answers with *It's . . . .* | 6 and 7 |
| **Vocabulary** | |
| ☐ say *hello* and *good-bye* in at least 4 different ways. | 1, 2, and 3 |
| ☐ talk about names in English. | 2 and 4 |
| ☐ use numbers 0–10. | 6 |
| **Conversation strategies** | |
| ☐ use *How about you?* | 8 |
| ☐ use everyday expressions in more formal and less formal situations. | 9 |

9

**1** ## Where is everybody today?

Grammar | **A** Look at the pictures. Complete the sentences.

1. Bill _'s_____ at the gym.
   _He's___ not at home.

2. Jon and Karen ___are___ at home. _____ not in class.

3. Sun-Yee _____ in the cafeteria. _____ late.

4. David _____ on vacation. _____ asleep.

5. Kate and Tess _____ in class. _____ not at the library.

6. Carmen _____ at work. _____ not sick.

**B** Complete the questions about the people in part A. Then answer the questions.

1. A _____Is____ Bill at work?
   B _No, he's not._____

2. A _____ Jon and Karen at home?
   B _____

3. A _____ Sun-Yee at the gym?
   B _____

4. A _____ David asleep?
   B _____

5. A _____ Kate and Tess on vacation?
   B _____

6. A _____ Carmen at work?
   B _____

# 2 Absent classmates

Grammar Complete the conversation with the verb *be*. Use contractions where possible. Add *not* where necessary.

Silvia   Hi. How ___*are*___ you?

Jason   Good, thanks. How about you?

Silvia   Pretty good. _____ Dave here?

Jason   No, he _____ _____ .
I think he _____ sick.

Silvia   Oh. _____ he at home?

Jason   I don't know.

Silvia   How about Jenny and Paula?
_____ they here?

Jason   No, they _____ _____ . They _____
on vacation. I think they _____ in Miami.

Silvia   Look! Dave _____ not sick. He _____ over
there. He _____ just late again!

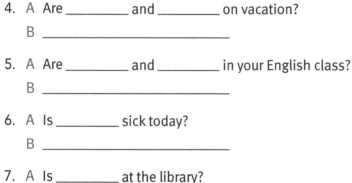

# 3 About you

Grammar and vocabulary Complete the questions with the names of your friends and classmates. Then answer the questions.

1. A   Is ___*Paul*___ at home?
   B   _*Yes, he is.*_____

2. A   Are _____ and _____ at work?
   B   _____

3. A   Is _____ in class today?
   B   _____

4. A   Are _____ and _____ on vacation?
   B   _____

5. A   Are _____ and _____ in your English class?
   B   _____

6. A   Is _____ sick today?
   B   _____

7. A   Is _____ at the library?
   B   _____

8. A   Are _____ and _____ asleep?
   B   _____

## 1 Everyday things

Vocabulary | Label the things in the pictures. Use *a* or *an* where necessary.

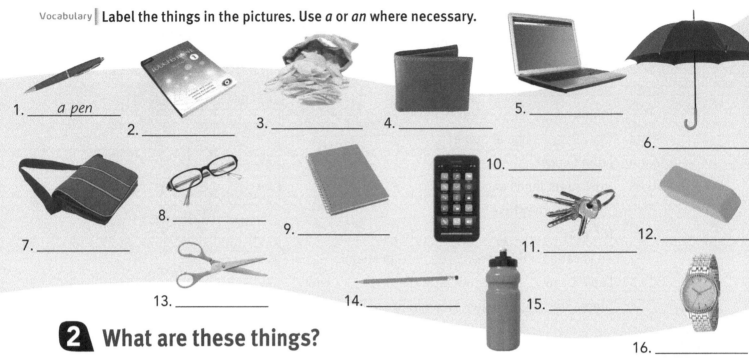

1. _____a pen_____
2. _____
3. _____
4. _____
5. _____
6. _____
7. _____
8. _____
9. _____
10. _____
11. _____
12. _____
13. _____
14. _____
15. _____
16. _____

## 2 What are these things?

Grammar and vocabulary | Write sentences about the pictures.

1. _____This is a bag._____
2. _____These are pens._____
3. _____
4. _____

5. _____
6. _____
7. _____
8. _____

# 3 Asking about things

Grammar | **Complete the conversations. Use the words in the box.**

| Is | it | it's | these | they're | this | What |
|----|----|------|-------|---------|------|------|
| Is | it's | these | they | they're | this | ✓ What's |

1. 
   **Clerk** You're in Room 102.

   **Ms. Simms** Thanks. *What's* this?

   **Clerk** Oh, _____ your room key.

   **Ms. Simms** OK. Thank you.

   **Clerk** And _____ is your membership card for the fitness club.

2. **Erica** What's _____ ? _____ it a smartphone?

   **Jim** No, _____ not. It's a GPS.

   **Erica** Oh.

   **Jim** _____ are these?

   **Erica** I think _____ watches.

3. **Bob** What are _____ ?

   **Jill** Oh, no! I think _____ my jeans.

   **Bob** Oh, I'm sorry. Are _____ new?

   **Jill** Yeah. Oh, look. _____ this your wallet?

   **Bob** Yes, _____ is.

   **Jill** Oh, no! And _____ are your credit cards!

13

## 1 Classroom things

Vocabulary | **A** Write the words under the pictures. Use *a* or *some*.

1. ___a board___

2. ___some posters___

3. _____

4. _____

5. _____

6. _____

7. _____

8. _____

9. _____

10. _____

11. _____

12. _____

**B** Circle the words from part A in the puzzle. Look in these directions (→ ↓). Which word is *not* in the puzzle?

| T | V | C | Q | U | A | B | L | A | M | A | B |
|---|---|---|---|---|---|---|---|---|---|---|---|
| W | E | H | A | S | I | P | U | Y | A | Z | O |
| A | C | A | L | E | N | D | A | R | P | H | A |
| G | O | I | H | K | O | B | Z | O | E | O | R |
| I | P | R | P | E | D | L | F | L | T | E | D |
| W | A | S | T | E | B | A | S | K | E | T | I |
| R | K | T | O | R | R | J | O | O | M | U | M |
| O | C | U | O | S | J | E | C | D | E | S | K |
| N | L | L | G | T | O | R | X | I | T | J | A |
| C | O | M | P | U | T | E | R | O | T | D | S |
| M | C | A | S | M | P | O | S | T | E | R | S |
| A | K | S | C | I | S | S | O | R | S | A | R |

# 2 A classroom

Grammar
and
vocabulary **A** Look at the picture. Complete the sentences. Use the words in the box.

| in | in front of | in front of | next to | ✓on | on | on | under |

1. The workbooks are ___on___ the table.
2. The calendar is _____ the wastebasket.
3. The computer is _____ the teacher's desk.
4. The map is _____ the window.

5. The students' papers are _____ the wall.
6. The teacher's desk is _____ the board.
7. The scissors are _____ the teacher's desk.
8. The table is _____ the chairs.

**B** Write the questions about the classroom in part A.

1. A _Where's the teacher's desk?_

   B It's in front of the board.

2. A _____

   B It's next to the window.

3. A _____

   B They're on the table.

4. A _____

   B They're under the teacher's desk.

5. A _____

   B They're on the wall.

6. A _____

   B It's in the wastebasket.

# 3 Missing apostrophes

Grammar Put apostrophes (') in the correct places in the questions. Then answer the questions.

1. What's on the wall in your classroom?   _____

2. What are your friends names?   _____

3. Whats your English teachers name?   _____

4. Wheres your teacher now?   _____

## 1 Questions, questions

**Conversation strategies** — Complete the conversations. Use the expressions in the box.

✓Excuse me    Thanks anyway.    Sure.    Here you go.    Thanks.
Can I borrow    You're welcome.    please    How do you spell    Sorry.
What's the word for this in English?

1.  Callie   _Excuse me_   , Bob.

    Bob   Yeah?

    Callie   _____ your English book?

    Bob   Sure. Now, where is it?

    Callie   Um . . . it's right in front of you.

    Bob   Oh, yeah. _____

    Callie   Thanks.

    Bob   _____

2.  Ruby   Can I borrow your cell phone,

             _____ ?

    Millie   _____ Oh, wait.

             It's not in my bag. I think it's at home.

             _____

    Ruby   That's OK. _____

    Millie   Sure. . . . _____

    Ruby   In English, the word is _umbrella_.

    Millie   Umbrella? Thanks.

    Ruby   Sure.

3.  Yuri   _____ _computers_?

    Dan   C-O-M-P-U-T-E-R-S.

    Yuri   _____

    Dan   Sure.

    Yuri   And how do you spell _television_?

    Dan   T-V.

    Yuri   Very funny!

## ❷ Scrambled conversations

Conversation strategies | **Number the lines of the conversations in the correct order. Then write the conversations.**

1. _____ I'm sorry.

   ___1___ You're late.

   _____ That's OK.

   A  *You're late.*_____

   B  _____

   A  _____


2. _____ Sure.

   _____ Thank you.

   _____ Can I borrow your pen, please?

   _____ You're welcome.

   A  _____

   B  _____

   A  _____

   B  _____


3. _____ I don't know.

   _____ That's OK. Thanks anyway.

   _____ That's OK. What about this?

   _____ I'm sorry. I don't know.

   _____ What's the word for this?

   A  _____

   B  _____

   A  _____

   B  _____

   A  _____


## Unit 2 Progress chart

| What can you do? Mark the boxes. ☑ = I can . . .    ? = I need to review how to . . . | To review, go back to these pages in the Student's Book. |
|---|---|
| ☐ make statements with *he's (not)*, *she's (not)*, and *they're (not)*. | 12 and 13 |
| ☐ ask questions with *Is he . . . ?*, *Is she . . . ?*, and *Are they . . . ?* | 13 |
| ☐ use *a* or *an*. | 14 |
| ☐ make nouns plural with *-s*, *-es*, or *-ies*. | 15 |
| ☐ use *this* with singular nouns and *these* with plural nouns. | 14 and 15 |
| ☐ ask questions with *Where . . . ?* | 17 |
| ☐ use *'s* and *s'* to show possession. | 17 |
| ☐ name at least 8 things students take to class. | 14 and 15 |
| ☐ name at least 12 classroom items. | 16 and 17 |
| ☐ say where things are in the classroom. | 16 and 17 |
| ☐ ask for help in class. | 18 |
| ☐ use common responses to *Thank you* and *I'm sorry*. | 19 |

Grammar — Vocabulary — Conversation strategies

17

# Favorite people

## Lesson A / Celebrities

### 1 Favorites

Vocabulary | **A** Unscramble the letters. Write the words.

1. rgiens   s_inger_
2. ctrao   a_____
3. rtweir   w_____
4. maet   t_____

5. ralype   p_____
6. dnab   b_____
7. prsot   s_____
8. naf   f_____

9. ivome   m_____
10. rtiats   a_____

**B** Complete the crossword puzzle with the words in part A.

|   |   |   |   |   |   |   | 1. |   |   |   |
|---|---|---|---|---|---|---|---|---|---|---|
|   |   |   | 2. |   |   |   |   |   |   |   |
|   |   |   |   |   |   |   |   |   |   |   |
|   |   | 3.| s | i | n | g | e | r |   |   |
|   | 4.|   |   |   |   | 5.|   | 6.|   |   |
| 7.|   |   |   |   |   |   |   |   |   |   |
| 8.|   |   |   |   |   |   |   |   |   |   |
|   |   |   |   |   |   | 9.|   |   |   |   |
|   |   |   |   | 10.|   |   |   |   |   |   |
|   |   |   |   |   |   |   |   |   |   |   |
|   |   |   |   |   |   |   |   |   |   |   |

**Across**

3. Adele is an amazing _____ .
5. Our favorite soccer _____ is Manchester United.
8. Hugh Jackman is a great _____ .
10. Ronaldo is a famous soccer _____ .

**Down**

1. Soccer is a _____ .
2. J.K. Rowling is a famous _____ .
4. Who's your favorite _____ ?
6. This _____ is exciting.
7. My favorite _____ is Coldplay.
9. Brian is a _____ of the Giants.

## 2 She's my favorite singer.

Grammar **Look at the pictures. Complete the sentences.**

1. " _She's_ my favorite singer. _Her_ new album is great."

2. "_____ Jama fans. Jama is _____ favorite band."

3. "_____ a great writer. _____ new book is really good."

4. "_____ favorite movie is *The Aliens*. What's _____ favorite movie?"

5. "_____ my favorite actors. I think _____ movies are very good."

6. "Cassandra Coe is my teacher. _____ a great artist. _____ pictures are amazing."

## 3 They're great!

Grammar **Complete the conversation with the verb *be*. Use contractions where possible.**

Alicia   I love this new Bruno Mars album. He _'s_ my favorite singer.

Norah   Yeah. I _____ a big fan of his, too. His voice _____ amazing. His songs _____ great.

Alicia   Yeah. So, what's your favorite band?

Norah   Maroon 5. They _____ great.

Alicia   Yes, they _____ very talented. Adam Levine _____ really good looking. He _____ my favorite.

## 1 What are they like?

Vocabulary Look at the pictures. Complete the sentences. Use the words in the box.

| busy | fun | | lazy | ✓quiet | smart | tired |
|------|-----|--|------|--------|-------|-------|
| friendly | interesting | outgoing | shy | strict | |

1. She's _____*quiet*_____ and _____ .

2. He's _____ .

3. They're _____ .

4. She's _____ .

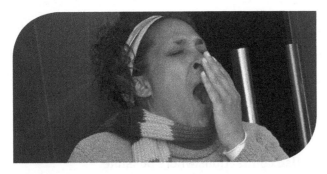

5. She's _____ .

6. He's _____ .

7. He's not very _____ or _____ .

8. They're _____ . She's _____ .

## 2  What's new?

Grammar Complete the conversation with the verb *be*. Use contractions where possible. Add *not* where necessary.

Carrie  Sorry. ___*Am*___ I late?

Josh  No, you ____ _____ . You ____ fine.

Carrie  Good. So, what's new? _____ you busy at work?

Josh  Yes, I _____ . Our boss _____ sick,
so he ____ _____ at work.

Carrie  Oh, really?

Josh  So, how about you? What _____ your new
neighbors like? _____ they nice?

Carrie  Yes, they _____ . They _____ OK.
They _____ very quiet.

Josh  _____ they students?

Carrie  No, they ____ _____ . The guy _____ a writer.

Josh  A writer? What about the woman? _____ she a writer, too?

Carrie  No, she ____ _____ . She ____ _____ a writer – she _____ a teacher. At our school!

## 3  Make it negative.

Grammar Rewrite the sentences in the negative form. Use contractions where possible.

1. My neighbors are very nice.  *My neighbors aren't very nice.*_____

2. My best friend is a student.  _____

3. I'm very shy.  _____

4. The students in my class are very smart.  _____

5. My English class is easy.  _____

6. My teacher is very quiet.  _____

## 4  About you

Grammar and vocabulary Complete the questions. Then write short answers. Add more information.

1. ___*Are*___ you outgoing?  *Yes, I am. I'm very outgoing.*_____

   **or**  *No, I'm not. I'm not outgoing.*_____

2. _____ your best friend lazy?  _____

3. _____ your English class hard?  _____

4. _____ your friends smart?  _____

5. _____ your teacher fun?  _____

6. _____ your classmates nice?  _____

7. _____ you tired today?  _____

8. _____ you and your friends busy after class?  _____

### 1 Who's who?

Vocabulary | Use the family tree to complete the sentences about this family.

1. David is Paul's _____son_____ .
2. John is Katy's _____ .
3. Katy is Paul's _____ .
4. Josh, David, and Emily are Paul and
   Katy's _____ .
5. Emily is Josh's _____ .
6. Josh is David's _____ .
7. John and Catherine are
   Katy's _____ .
8. Katy is Josh's _____ .
9. John is Catherine's _____ .
10. Emily is Katy's _____ .
11. Catherine is David's _____ .
12. John is Emily's _____ .
13. Susan is David's _____ .
14. Bill is Josh's _____ .
15. Robert is Emily's _____ .

### 2 What's the number?

Vocabulary | Write the numbers.

**65**

1. ____sixty-five____

**11**

2. _____

**24**

3. _____

**15**

4. _____

**16**

5. _____

**91**

6. _____

**56**

7. _____

**77**

8. _____

# 3 How about your children?

Grammar and vocabulary Complete the conversations. Write the full questions.

1. A How / your parents?

   *How are your parents?*

   B They're fine. Thanks. How / your mom?

   _____

   A She's good. She's on vacation right now.

2. A What / your sisters' names?

   _____

   B Beth and Kate. My brother's name is Pete.

   A Pete? Oh, how old / he?

   _____

   B He's 21.

3. A Who / this?

   _____

   B Oh, it's my aunt.

4. A My cousins are really fun.

   B Yeah? How old / they?

   _____

   A They're my age.

5. A Where / your family today?

   _____

   B At home. How about your family?

   A They're at home, too.

6. A Where / you from?

   _____

   B Well, my parents are from Italy originally.

   A Really? Where / your parents from in Italy?

   _____

   B They're from Rome.

# 4 A famous family

Grammar Read part of a phone interview with an actor. Then write questions for the answers.

| | |
|---|---|
| Interviewer | Hello, Kate. How are you? |
| Kate | Hi. I'm fine, thanks. |
| Interviewer | Kate, I love your movies. |
| Kate | Thank you. |
| Interviewer | Now, about your family . . . who's your mother? |
| Kate | Gwen Russell – the artist. And Kevin Russell is my father. |
| Interviewer | Yes, they're famous! What are your parents like at home? |
| Kate | Oh, Dad's fun and outgoing. And Mom's very smart! |
| Interviewer | And, Kate, what's your favorite band? |
| Kate | Imagine Dragons. They're amazing. . . . |

1. *How is Kate?*_____

   She's fine.

2. _____

   Her mother is Gwen Russell.

3. _____

   Her father is fun and outgoing. Her mother is very smart.

4. _____

   Her favorite band is Imagine Dragons.

## 1 New neighbors and co-workers

Conversation strategies | **Complete the conversations with the questions in the box.**

| How old is she? | Where is she from? | ✓What are they like? | An actor? Is she good? |
| From Chile? | Are they friendly? | Are they good? | Where are they from? |

1. **Ming**    Who are they?

   **Jim**    Oh, they're my new neighbors.

   **Ming**    Your neighbors? _What are they like?_

   **Jim**    Interesting. Very interesting. They're in a
   rock band.

   **Ming**    A rock band? _____

   **Jim**    They're from New York.

   **Ming**    Wow! _____

   **Jim**    No, they're not.

   **Ming**    Uh-oh. _____

   **Jim**    Oh, very. Their friends are always here!

2. **Carlos**    Who's she?

   **Kim**    Her name's Angie.

   **Carlos**    Angie? _____

   **Kim**    I don't know exactly. I think she's from Chile.

   **Carlos**    _____ Really?

   What's she like?

   **Kim**    She's outgoing and fun.

   **Carlos**    Really? _____

   **Kim**    I'm not sure. Maybe 24 or 25.

   **Carlos**    Oh. What's her job? Is she a server here?

   **Kim**    Well, yes. But she's an actor, too.

   **Carlos**    _____

   **Kim**    Yeah, she's a good actor but not a great server.

# 2 Really? I'm surprised!

**Write responses to show you are interested or surprised. Then ask a question.**

1. My grandmother's name is Banu.    *Really? What's she like?*

2. My brother is a singer in a band.

3. My grandfather is a tennis player.

4. I'm from Alaska.

5. My mother is a Spanish teacher.

6. My new job is hard work.

7. My sister is an artist.

8. My last name is Oh.

## Unit 3 Progress chart

| What can you do? Mark the boxes.<br>☑ = I can . . .          ? = I need to review how to . . . | To review, go back to these pages in the Student's Book. |
|---|---|
| ☐ use *my*, *your*, *his*, *her*, *our*, and *their*. | 22 and 23 |
| ☐ make statements with *be*. | 22 and 23 |
| ☐ ask *yes-no* questions with *be*. | 24 and 25 |
| ☐ make negative statements with *be*. | 24 and 25 |
| ☐ ask information questions with *be*. | 26 and 27 |
| ☐ name at least 8 words to describe people's personalities. | 24 and 25 |
| ☐ name at least 12 family words. | 26 and 27 |
| ☐ say numbers 10–101. | 26 |
| ☐ show interest by repeating information and asking questions. | 28 |
| ☐ use *Really?* to show interest or surprise. | 29 |

Grammar

Vocabulary

Conversation strategies

# Everyday life

 **What's Kathy's morning like?**

Grammar
and
vocabulary

**A** Complete the sentences about Kathy's morning. Use the correct form of the verbs in the box.

| check | exercise | ✓get up | play |
|-------|----------|---------|------|
| eat | get up | listen | read |

1. Kathy __gets up__ early. Her son _____ late.

2. She _____ before work. Her son _____ games.

3. She _____ to the radio in the car.

4. She and her co-workers _____ breakfast together.

5. Kathy _____ her email right after breakfast.

6. Her boss _____ the newspaper at work.

**B** Rewrite the sentences in the negative form. Use contractions where possible.

1. Kathy's son gets up early. _Kathy's son doesn't get up early._____

2. Kathy checks her email before breakfast. _____

3. Kathy and her son talk a lot in the morning. _____

4. Kathy's son does his homework. _____

5. Kathy and her boss eat breakfast together. _____

6. Kathy's boss plays computer games. _____

## 2 Guess what!

Grammar | Complete Peter's email with the correct form of the verbs.

```
New Message                                    ⊟ ☐ ✕

    To: Samir22@cup.com
  From: PeterJ@cup.com
Subject: New Job

Hi!
Guess what! I ___have___ (have) a new job – in a coffee shop. It's hard work. I _____ (get up) early,
and I _____ (work) late. But the coffee is good.
My boss is nice. He's French, and he _____ (study) English at night. He _____ (do) his
homework in the coffee shop. I _____ (help) him
sometimes. He's quiet, and he _____ (not / talk) a lot. He
_____ (listen) to the radio and _____ (sing), but we
_____ (not / like) the same music. He _____ (like)
coffee, too. We both _____ (have) four cups of coffee
every day!
Write soon!
Peter
```

## 3 Typical morning activities

Grammar and vocabulary | **A** What are typical morning activities? Match the verbs with the words and expressions.

1. do __d__
2. study _____
3. check _____
4. listen _____
5. drive _____
6. play _____
7. read _____
8. go _____

a. to the radio
b. (my) email or messages
c. a car
✓d. (my) homework
e. on the Internet
f. English
g. games on the computer
h. a book

**B** Write true sentences about your morning routine. Use the verbs in part A.

1. _I don't do my homework in the morning._
2. _____
3. _____
4. _____
5. _____
6. _____
7. _____
8. _____

## 1 What's fun? What's not?

Vocabulary | **A** Which routine activities are fun for you? Complete the charts. Add your own ideas.

| | | | |
|---|---|---|---|
| check email | do the laundry | go shopping | take a class |
| clean the house | eat snacks | make phone calls | text friends |
| do homework | get up early | ✓ play sports | watch TV |

| Fun! | |
|---|---|
| *play sports* | |
| | |
| | |
| | |

| Not fun! | |
|---|---|
| | |
| | |
| | |
| | |

**B** Write the days of the week in the date book. Then write one thing you do each day.

S*unday* : *I go shopping on Sundays.*    Th_____ : _____
M_____ : _____    F_____ : _____
T_____ : _____    S_____ : _____
W_____ : _____

## 2 About you 1

Grammar and vocabulary | Use time expressions to write one thing you do and one thing you don't do.

1. on the weekends    *I clean the house on the weekends.*
                       *I don't go to work on the weekends.*

2. after work / class  _____
                       _____

3. every day           _____
                       _____

4. on Saturdays        _____
                       _____

5. in the afternoons   _____
                       _____

6. at night            _____
                       _____

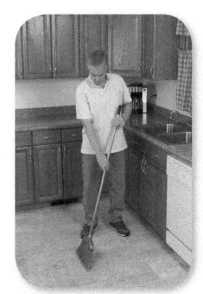

## 3 What's your week like?

**Grammar** Complete the conversation with the correct form of the verbs.

Cecilia   What's your week like, Eduardo? __*Do*__
          (Do / Does)

          you ___*go*___ to work every day?
          (go / goes)

Eduardo   Well, no, I _____ . I work at home on Fridays.
          (don't / doesn't)

Cecilia   Really? What about on the weekends? _____
          (Do / Does)

          you _____ then, too?
          (work / works)

Eduardo   Yes, I _____ . But I don't like it. What
          (do / does)

          about you? _____ you and your husband
          (Do / Does)

          _____ to work every day?
          (go / goes)

Cecilia   Yes, we _____ . But just Monday to Friday.
          (do / does)

          We _____ the house on the weekends.
          (clean / cleans)

          Oh, and we _____ to soccer games.
          ( go / goes)

Eduardo   Oh. _____ your son _____ soccer?
          (Do / Does)        (play / plays)

Cecilia   Yes, he _____ . He's on the school team.
          (do / does)

          _____ your son _____ any sports?
          (Do / Does)        (play / plays)

Eduardo   No, he _____ . He plays games on his computer.
          (don't / doesn't)

## 4 About you 2

**Grammar and vocabulary** Complete the questions. Then write answers with your own information.

1. A ___*Do*___ you ___*take*___ a class at night?
   B *Yes, I do. I take a Spanish class on Monday evenings.* _____

2. A _____ your father _____ the laundry on weekends?
   B _____

3. A _____ you and your friends _____ shopping on Saturdays?
   B _____

4. A _____ your friends _____ their email before breakfast?
   B _____

5. A _____ your mother _____ the news on the Internet every day?
   B _____

## 1 Saying more than *yes* or *no*

**A** Complete the conversation. Use the sentences in the box.

> I work part-time in the cafeteria.    It's fun, and the people are nice.
> Just Mondays and Wednesdays.    I'm an English student.
> ✓ I'm new here, and I'm late.    I go there Mondays after work. It's great!

**Mike**   Hi. Are you OK? You look lost.

**Yumi**   Hello. Where's Room 106? Do you know?
     *I'm new here, and I'm late.*

**Mike**   Yeah. It's right over there, next to the cafeteria.

**Yumi**   Thanks. So, do you work here?

**Mike**   Yes, I do. _____

**Yumi**   Do you like the job?

**Mike**   Yeah, I do. _____

**Yumi**   That's good. Do you work here every day?

**Mike**   Well, no. _____

     I go to class on Tuesdays and Thursdays.

**Yumi**   Oh. So you're a student, too?

**Mike**   Yeah. _____

**Yumi**   Really? I'm an English student, too. Do you belong
to the English Club?

**Mike**   Yes, I do. _____

**Yumi**   Oh. Well, thanks a lot. And see you at English Club!

**Mike**   Great!

**B** Read the completed conversation again. Then read the sentences below.
Check (✓) *T* (true) or *F* (false).

| | T | F |
|---|---|---|
| 1. Mike and Yumi are friends. | ☐ | ✓ |
| 2. Mike works in the cafeteria. | ☐ | ☐ |
| 3. Mike is a new student. | ☐ | ☐ |
| 4. Mike works Tuesdays and Thursdays. | ☐ | ☐ |
| 5. Mike likes his part-time job. | ☐ | ☐ |
| 6. Yumi and Mike are English students. | ☐ | ☐ |
| 7. Mike belongs to the English Club. | ☐ | ☐ |

## 2 About you

Unscramble the questions. Then answer the questions. Write more than
*yes* or *no*. Use *Well* if you need to.

1. live / you / around / Do / here ?

   *Do you live around here?*

2. from / originally / you / here / Are ?

3. a / full-time / you / Are / student ?

4. have / you / brothers / Do / sisters / or ?

5. you / work / the / on / weekends / Do ?

6. Do / your / every day / text / friends / you ?

7. get up / day / you / Do / every / early ?

8. grandparents / Do / with / your / live / you ?

## 1 Watching TV

**A** What do you think average Americans do after work and school? Check (✓) three boxes.

☐ spend time with family ☐ read ☐ watch TV
☐ go out with friends ☐ go out to dinner ☐ go shopping

**B** Read the article. Check your answers in part A.

## After WORK and SCHOOL

Do Americans go out every night after work and have fun? Maybe the answer is surprising, but no, they don't. They don't usually go out with friends in the evening, and they don't go out to dinner or go shopping. So what do they do? Well, about 90% of Americans stay at home in the evening to relax. In fact, it's their favorite activity. They read, watch TV, and spend time with their families.

So what about young people? Well, they spend a lot of time at home, too. American high school students study about six hours a week and watch TV for about 15 hours a week.

Most Americans also have a hobby and do fun, interesting things like play sports or music. Americans stay home a lot, but they stay busy, too!

Here are average Americans' favorite activities:

- reading
- watching TV
- spending time with their families
- exercising
- using the Internet

**C** Read the article again. Then correct these false sentences.

1. Americans go out with friends every night after work.
   _Americans don't usually go out with friends in the evening._

2. After work, Americans usually go shopping.
   _____

3. American high school students usually study for three hours a night.
   _____

4. American high school students don't watch TV.
   _____

5. The average American doesn't have a hobby.
   _____

# 2 Weekends

Writing **A** Read the email messages. Then rewrite Joe's message. Use capital letters and periods.

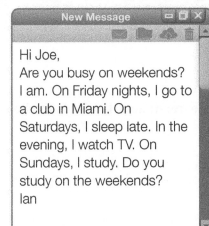

Hi Joe,
Are you busy on weekends?
I am. On Friday nights, I go to
a club in Miami. On
Saturdays, I sleep late. In the
evening, I watch TV. On
Sundays, I study. Do you
study on the weekends?
Ian

hi ian,
yes, i have busy weekends on
friday nights, i visit my family
downtown on saturdays,
i take a spanish class at grove
college on sundays, i play
soccer i don't study on
weekends – i don't have time
joe

*Hi Ian,*
_____
_____
_____
_____
_____
_____
_____
_____

**B** What do you do on weekends? Write an email to a friend about your weekend activities.

Hi _____ ,
_____
_____
_____
_____
_____
_____

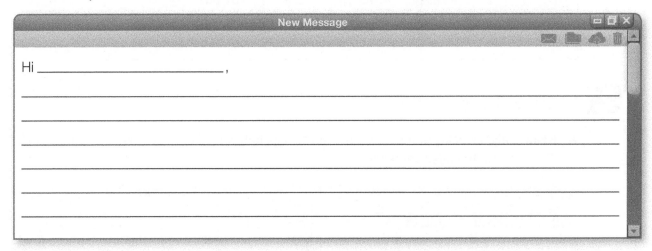

## Unit 4 Progress chart

| What can you do? Mark the boxes.  ☑ = I can . . .        ? = I need to review how to . . . | To review, go back to these pages in the Student's Book. |
|---|---|
| Grammar | |
| ☐ make simple present statements. | 34 and 35 |
| ☐ ask simple present *yes-no* questions and give short answers. | 36 and 37 |
| Vocabulary | |
| ☐ name at least 12 new verbs for routine activities. | 34, 35, 36, and 37 |
| ☐ name the days of the week. | 36 |
| ☐ name at least 8 time expressions with the simple present. | 37 |
| Conversation strategies | |
| ☐ answer questions with more than *yes* or *no*. | 38 and 39 |
| ☐ use *Well* to get time to think of an answer. | 39 |
| Writing | |
| ☐ use capital letters and periods. | 41 |

# Free time

## Lesson A / Going out

### 1 In your free time

Vocabulary | How often do you do these things? Complete the chart with the free-time activities in the box. Add your own ideas.

| ✓ eat out | go out with friends | go to a club | go to the gym | play a sport |
|-----------|---------------------|--------------|---------------|--------------|
| go on the Internet | go shopping | go to a movie | have dinner with family | text family |

| every day | three or four times a week | once or twice a week | once or twice a month |
|-----------|----------------------------|----------------------|------------------------|
| | | eat out | |
| | | | |
| | | | |

### 2 Craig's busy schedule

Grammar and vocabulary | **A** Read Craig's weekly planner. Are the sentences below true or false? Write *T* (true) or *F* (false). Then correct the false sentences.

**WEEKLY PLANNER**

| SUNDAY | MONDAY | TUESDAY | WEDNESDAY | THURSDAY | FRIDAY | SATURDAY |
|--------|--------|---------|-----------|----------|--------|----------|
| **5** | **6** | **7** | **8** | **9** | **10** | **11** |
| **morning:** *do the laundry!!* | **morning:** *classes* | **morning:** *go to the gym!* | **morning:** *classes* | **morning:** *go to the gym!* | **morning:** *classes* | **morning:** *clean the house!!* |
| | **afternoon:** *go shopping* | **afternoon:** *library* | **afternoon:** *guitar lesson* | | | **afternoon:** *tennis with Bob* |
| **evening:** *dinner with Mom and Dad* | | | | **evening:** *dinner with Sandra* | **evening:** *movie with Jim* | **evening:** *club with Bill* |

*three evenings a week*

1. He goes out with friends ~~every evening.~~ __F__

2. He goes to the library every day. _____

3. He goes shopping once a week. _____

4. He takes guitar lessons on Wednesday mornings. _____

5. He plays tennis twice a week. _____

6. He does the laundry three times a week. _____

7. He sees his parents on the weekends. _____

8. He cleans the house on Saturday mornings. _____

Grammar **B   Now answer these questions about Craig's schedule.**

1.  How often does he go to the gym?      *He goes to the gym twice a week.* _____

2.  When does he have classes?      _____

3.  How often does he go to a club?      _____

4.  What does he do on Thursday evenings?      _____

5.  When does he go to the movies?      _____

6.  What does he do on Saturday afternoons?      _____

7.  Who does he play tennis with?      _____

8.  Where does he go on Saturday evenings?      _____

# 3   About you

Grammar
and
vocabulary    **Write questions for a friend. Then answer your friend's questions.**

1.   You    *Where do you go after class?* _____
(go after class)

   Friend   I meet some friends and go to a restaurant for dinner.
   How about you?

   You    _____

2.   You    _____
(text your friends)

   Friend   Every day.  But I don't text before breakfast. How about you?

   You    _____

3.   You    _____
(do in your free time at home)

   Friend   I rent a movie, or I just relax in front of the TV with a friend.
   How about you?

   You    _____

4.   You    _____
(go on the weekends)

   Friend   I go to a restaurant or club. How about you?

   You    _____

5.   You    _____
(go out with)

   Friend   Oh, friends from school. How about you?

   You    _____

## 1 How often?

Grammar **A** Write the frequency adverbs in order in the chart below.

✓always    hardly ever    never    often    sometimes    usually

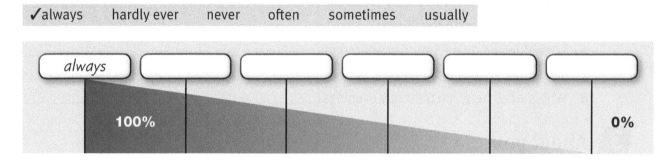

| always | | | | | |

100%                                                                    0%

**B** Answer the questions. Write true sentences using frequency adverbs.

**What's something you . . .**

1. hardly ever do before school or work?  *I hardly ever check my email before school.*

2. always do in the morning?  _____

3. sometimes do after school or work?  _____

4. never do during dinner?  _____

5. often do in the evening?  _____

6. usually do on Saturdays?  _____

## 2 What kinds of TV shows do you know?

Vocabulary **A** Look at the pictures. Circle the correct type of TV show.

1. (soap opera)/ the news

2. talk show / cartoon

3. sitcom / the news

4. cartoon / game show

5. documentary / talk show

6. talk show / cartoon

7. sitcom / reality show

8. the news / game show

**B** Circle the kinds of TV shows from part A in the puzzle. Look in these directions (→↓).

| T | C | S | I | T | C | O | M | E | T | I | S |
|---|---|---|---|---|---|---|---|---|---|---|---|
| E | A | O | E | D | H | P | O | R | H | I | H |
| L | R | E | A | L | I | T | Y | S | H | O | W |
| K | T | A | L | K | S | H | O | W | U | P | O |
| S | O | A | P | O | P | E | R | A | E | E | U |
| D | O | C | U | M | E | N | T | A | R | Y | N |
| A | N | O | O | T | H | E | J | E | I | W | S |
| Y | T | E | A | I | U | W | D | O | C | T | V |
| Y | C | G | A | M | E | S | H | O | W | L | Y |

# 3 About you

Grammar
and
vocabulary

**Answer the questions. Give two pieces of your own information in each answer.**

1. Do you ever watch soap operas? _Yes, I usually watch soap operas in the afternoons._
   _I love the stories._

2. What sitcoms do you hardly ever watch? _____
   _____

3. How often do you watch documentaries? _____
   _____

4. What talk shows do you like? _____
   _____

5. When do you usually watch the news? _____
   _____

6. How often do you watch reality shows? _____
   _____

## 1 Asking questions in two ways

Conversation strategies | **Complete the conversations with the questions in the box.**

| | |
|---|---|
| Do you like French? | I mean, do you belong to any clubs? |
| ✓ Do you do anything special? | I mean, do you know a nice place? |
| Do you play baseball? | I mean, do you go every day? |

1. Lisa   What do you do after work?
          *Do you do anything special?*

   Debbie   Well, I go to the gym.

   Lisa   Really? How often do you go?
   _____

   Debbie   No, not every day. I go Mondays, Wednesdays, and Thursdays.

2. Howard   Do you know the restaurants around here?
   _____

   Mary   Well, I often go to a little place on Main Street. What kind of food do you like?
   _____

   Howard   Yes, I do. I love French food.

3. Paul   What do you do after school?
   _____

   Tom   Well, yeah. I'm in the Sports Club.
   Paul   Really? What do you play?
   _____

   Tom   Well, no. We watch baseball on TV!
   Paul   Oh.

# 2 Questions, questions

Conversation strategies | Write a second question for each question below. Then write true answers.

1. What's your teacher like?
   *I mean, is she nice?*
   *Yes, she's very nice. She's friendly.*

2. How often do you have English class?
   _____

3. How do you get to school / work?
   _____

4. What do you do for fun on the weekends?
   _____

5. Do you read a lot?
   _____

6. Do you ever go to clubs?
   _____

# 3 About you

Conversation strategies | Add frequency adverbs to make these sentences true for you.
Then use *I mean*, and write more information.

1. I _never_ go to the gym. *I mean, I usually exercise at home.*
2. I _____ get home early. _____
3. I _____ see my friends during the week. _____
4. I _____ go on the Internet in the evening. _____
5. I _____ eat breakfast at school / work. _____
6. I _____ get up early. _____
7. I _____ eat out on Saturdays. _____
8. I _____ watch reality shows on TV. _____
9. I _____ go shopping on the weekends. _____
10. I _____ study English after dinner. _____

## 1 Paula's problem

Reading **A** Read Paula's post to an online forum. How many hours does Paula spend online?

☐ 3 or 4 hours          ☐ 4 or 5 hours          ☐ 8 or 9 hours

---

**PaulaT18**   posted 2 hours ago

I live with my parents and my two brothers. They say I hardly ever spend time with them. My parents say I spend too much time on my phone and in front of my computer, but I don't think that's true. I mean, I often get up early and check my messages, but we always eat breakfast together. I guess I sometimes text during breakfast, but I never call people then. After class, I listen to music on my phone, but I also do my homework. In the evening, I often log on to my social network to chat with friends. They're always online. Sometimes I watch a movie on my computer. I usually spend eight or nine hours online every day. I don't think it's a problem. What do you think?

---

**B** Read Paula's post again. Then answer the questions.

1. Who does Paula live with? *She lives with her parents and her two brothers.*

2. Is she a student? _____

   _____

3. When does she log on to her social network? _____

   _____

4. What does Paula use her phone and computer for? _____

   _____

   _____

5. What do you think? Does Paula have a problem? Why or why not?

   _____

   _____

   _____

# 2 I need some advice!

**A  Read José's post to an online forum. Complete it with *and* or *but*.**

José    posted 2 hours ago
_____

I think I have a problem. I don't have a computer at home, ___*but*___ I use a computer at
school. I usually go to school early, _____ I check my email. I send email to my friends in
other countries. I often go online for fun, _____ sometimes I study English on the computer.
Then on the weekends, I go to school _____ write papers for class (on the computer). Do I
spend too much time at school?

**B  Write a post for an online forum about a problem you have. Write about a problem below,
or use your own idea.**

"I watch too much TV."          "I go shopping too much."          "I work too much."

"I stay home too much."         "I talk on my cell phone too much."          "I study too much."

_____
_____
_____
_____
_____
_____

## Unit 5 Progress chart

| What can you do? Mark the boxes. ✓ = I can . . .          ? = I need to review how to . . . | To review, go back to these pages in the Student's Book. |
|---|---|
| **Grammar** | |
| ☐ ask simple present information questions. | 44 and 45 |
| ☐ use time expressions like *once a week*. | 44 and 45 |
| ☐ use frequency adverbs like *sometimes*, *never*, etc. | 46 |
| **Vocabulary** | |
| ☐ name at least 6 new free-time activities. | 44 and 45 |
| ☐ name at least 6 kinds of TV shows. | 47 |
| ☐ talk about likes and dislikes. | 47 |
| **Conversation strategies** | |
| ☐ ask questions in 2 ways to be less direct. | 48 |
| ☐ use *I mean* to repeat an idea and say more. | 49 |
| **Writing** | |
| ☐ use *and* and *but* to link ideas. | 51 |

## 1 What's in the neighborhood?

Vocabulary | Label the places in the picture. Use the words in the box with *a / an* or *some*.

| | | | | | |
|---|---|---|---|---|---|
| ✓apartment buildings | fast-food places | museum | park | restaurants | supermarket |
| club | movie theater | outdoor café | post office | stores | swimming pool |

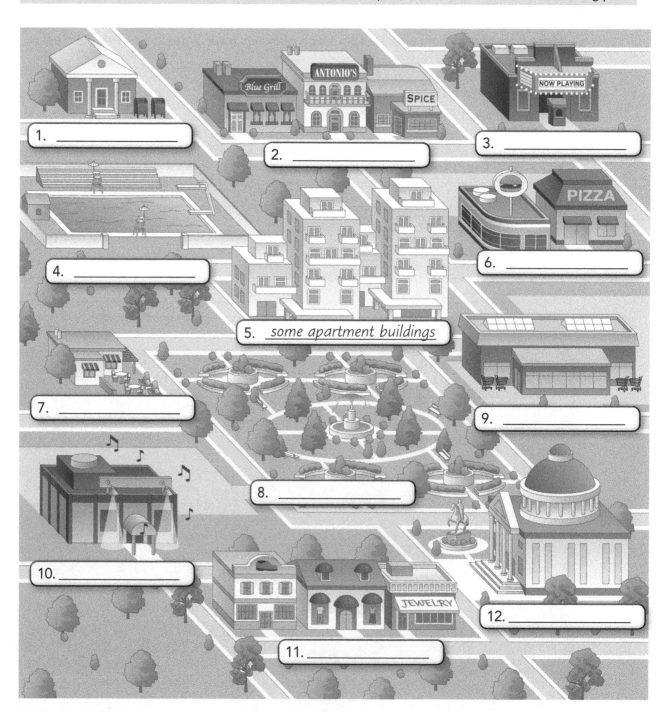

1. _____
2. _____
3. _____
4. _____
5. _*some apartment buildings*_
6. _____
7. _____
8. _____
9. _____
10. _____
11. _____
12. _____

# 2 Can you find the opposites?

Vocabulary | **Find six pairs of adjective opposites in the box. Write them in the chart below.**

| bad | boring | expensive | interesting | noisy | quiet |
|-----|--------|-----------|-------------|-------|-------|
| big | cheap | good | ✓ new | ✓ old | small |

| |
|---|
| *new — old* |
| |
| |
| |
| |
| |

# 3 That's not quite right!

Grammar | **Look at the picture on page 42. Correct the sentences to describe the neighborhood.**

1. There's one cheap fast-food place.     *There are a couple of cheap fast-food places.*

2. There are a couple of post offices. _____

3. There's a big stadium. _____

4. There are a couple of supermarkets. _____

5. There are some malls. _____

6. There's an apartment building. _____

7. There are no small stores. _____

8. There's an expensive restaurant. _____

9. There are a lot of beautiful parks. _____

10. There's no movie theater. _____

# 4 About you

Grammar and vocabulary | **What's your neighborhood like? Complete the sentences with true information.**

1. There's a _____ .

2. There are a lot of _____ .

3. There are some _____ .

4. There are a couple of _____ .

5. There's no _____ .

6. There are no _____ .

## 1 What's the time?

Vocabulary **A** Write the times in words. Where there are two lines, write the times two ways.

1. It's twelve p.m.

   It's noon.

2. _____

   _____

3. _____

4. _____

5. _____

   _____

6. _____

   _____

**B** Read about Kayo's day. Write the times in numbers. Then number the sentences in the correct order.

_____ Her bus comes at __7:55__ (five to eight).

_____ She gets home at _____ (nine fifteen) and watches TV.

__1__ Kayo gets up at _____ (six twenty-five).

_____ She goes for lunch with her co-workers at _____ (noon).

_____ She starts work at _____ (eight forty-five).

_____ She meets her boyfriend at _____ (twenty five to six), and they have dinner.

_____ She eats breakfast at _____ (twenty after seven).

_____ She leaves work at _____ (ten after five).

_____ She goes to bed at _____ (ten thirty).

## 2  Let's do it!

Grammar **Complete the conversations. Write questions starting with *What time . . . ?*
Use *Let's* to end each conversation with a suggestion.**

1. A  I'm starving. Let's go to Burger Queen.
   B  But it's late. *What time does it close?*
   A  It closes around 11:00, I think. _____
   B  Almost 10:00. _____

2. A  There's a new reality show on TV tonight.
   B  _____
   A  Um, I think it starts at 8:00.
   B  Well, I'm really tired. _____
   A  I'm not sure. I think it ends at 9:30.
   B  OK. _____

3. A  Let's go to the gym on Saturday morning.
   B  Sure. _____
   A  Oh, it opens early. At 6:00. _____
   B  I usually get up around 8:00 on Saturdays.
   A  OK. _____

## 3  About you

Grammar
and
vocabulary **Unscramble the questions. Then write true answers.**

1. do / What time / get up / on weekdays / you ?
   A  *What time do you get up on weekdays?*
   B  _____

2. your family / have / What time / does / lunch / on Sundays ?
   A  _____
   B  _____

3. your English class / What time / start / does ?
   A  _____
   B  _____

4. What time / leave home / do / you / in the morning ?
   A  _____
   B  _____

5. stores / do / What time / in your neighborhood / open and close ?
   A  _____
   B  _____

## 1 Responses

Conversation strategies
**Circle the two correct responses to each comment. Cross out the incorrect response.**

1. I think every neighborhood needs a park.
   a. ~~Me neither.~~
   b. (Me too.)
   c. (Right.)

2. We don't have a good fast-food place here.
   a. Yeah.
   b. Me too.
   c. I know.

3. I don't like the new restaurant.
   a. Yeah. I know.
   b. Me neither.
   c. Me too.

4. There are no good bookstores around here.
   a. I know.
   b. Me too.
   c. Right.

5. I like the new outdoor café downtown.
   a. Me neither.
   b. Me too.
   c. Right. It's good.

6. I love this neighborhood. It's so quiet.
   a. Right.
   b. Yeah, I know.
   c. Me neither.

## 2 What do they have in common?

Conversation strategies
**Read the conversation. Are the sentences below true or false? Write *T* (true) or *F* (false).**

**Glen** What's your new neighborhood like?

**Anna** Oh, it's amazing. There are a lot of outdoor cafés and movie theaters and clubs. I go out a lot.

**Glen** Really? I hardly ever go out in my neighborhood. It's boring.

**Anna** Let's do something in my neighborhood this weekend. I'm free on Saturday.

**Glen** Me too.

**Anna** Well, there's a great jazz club near my apartment. I love jazz.

**Glen** Really? Me too!

**Anna** But let's have dinner at a café first. The food at the club is expensive, and I don't have a lot of money.

**Glen** Me neither. So, let's meet at 6:30 at your apartment.

1. Glen and Anna both like their neighborhoods.  _F_

2. Glen and Anna both go out a lot in their neighborhoods. _____

3. Glen and Anna are both free on Saturday. _____

4. Glen and Anna both love jazz. _____

5. Glen and Anna both have a lot of money. _____

> **Help note**
>
> Glen and Anna **both** love jazz.
> Glen loves jazz, **and** Anna loves jazz, **too**.

## 3 Right. I know.

Circle the expression that is true about your neighborhood. Then show you agree. Respond with *Right* or *I know*.

1. A (There are some)/ **There are no** good restaurants in my neighborhood.

   B _I know._

2. A My neighborhood **has / doesn't have** a lot of great stores.

   B _____

3. A I live in a **great / terrible** neighborhood.

   B _____

4. A We **need / don't need** a shopping mall around here.

   B _____

## 4 About you

Imagine you're talking to people from your neighborhood. Write true responses.

1. I really like this neighborhood.

   *Me too. I think it's great.* _____
   **or**
   *Really? I don't like it very much.* _____

2. I don't eat out in this neighborhood.

3. I think the restaurants are very expensive here.

4. I don't know a lot of people around here.

5. I think our neighborhood is boring.

6. I think we need a couple of new stores in our neighborhood.

# 1 Free weekend events!

Reading **A** Read about some local events on a website. Match the pictures with the events. Write the correct numbers next to the pictures.

### Downtown Weekend Section

### * * * FREE EVENTS * * *

**1. All Day Music** Meet local bands, singers, and musicians at City Park this Sunday. Listen to great music, dance to pop songs, or take a music workshop and write your own song! The music starts at 3 p.m. and finishes at 11 p.m. Call Melissa at 555-9075 for more information.

**2. Spring Food Festival** Do you love food? Do you often eat out? Then come to the Parkview Food Festival. Eat some delicious food from 20 different restaurants around the neighborhood – all for FREE! *Saturday from 11:00 a.m. to 4:00 p.m. at Green Street Park.*

**3. Outdoor Street Fair** *Saturday and Sunday from 10:00 a.m. to 6:00 p.m. in front of the City Art Museum.* There are a lot of beautiful items for sale – books, art, photos, paintings, clothes, and more. Items for sale are just $2–$25. Coffee, sodas, and snacks are for sale, too!

**4. Free Classes at the Neighborhood Center** Do you want to take a class but don't have the time? Try a free one-hour class Monday through Friday this week. Learn:
- Art
- Spanish
- Music
- French
- Computers
- Yoga

Classes start at 10:00 a.m. and 2:00 p.m. Go to www.freeclass.cup.org for more information.

**B** Read the website again. Then answer the questions. Check (✓) the correct events.

| Which events . . . | The concert | The food festival | The street fair | The free classes |
|---|---|---|---|---|
| 1. have food? | ☐ | ✓ | ✓ | ☐ |
| 2. are on Saturday? | ☐ | ☐ | ☐ | ☐ |
| 3. have a website? | ☐ | ☐ | ☐ | ☐ |
| 4. are during the day? | ☐ | ☐ | ☐ | ☐ |
| 5. are at night? | ☐ | ☐ | ☐ | ☐ |
| 6. are outdoors? | ☐ | ☐ | ☐ | ☐ |

## 2 Make your own event.

Writing **A** Complete the sentences with the prepositions in the box.

| at | at | at | between | for | ✓from | on | through | to |
|---|---|---|---|---|---|---|---|---|

1. The event is __*from*__ 6:00 _____ 10:00.

2. The event is _____ 8:00 p.m. _____ the stadium _____ Main Street.

3. Go to www.eventinfo.cup.org _____ more information, or call Jim _____ 555-7777.

4. Call _____ 12:00 p.m. and 5:00 p.m., Monday _____ Friday.

**B** Imagine you are planning an event. Answer the questions. Use the ideas in the boxes and your own ideas.

| Events: | Places: |
|---|---|
| a play, an art exhibit, a concert, a sports event | the library, the museum, the park, the theater |

1. What is the event? _____

2. When and where is it? _____

3. What time does it start and finish? _____

4. What's the cost of the event? Is it free? _____

5. What things are there to do at the event? _____

6. Where or how do people get more information? _____

**C** Write an ad for an event in your town or city. Give the event a name.

_____

_____

_____

## Unit 6 Progress chart

| What can you do? Mark the boxes.<br>✓ = I can . . .          ? = I need to review how to . . . | To review, go back to these pages in the Student's Book. |
|---|---|
| ☐ use *There's* and *There are* with singular and plural nouns. | 54 and 55 |
| ☐ use quantifiers *a lot of*, *some*, *a couple of*, and *no*. | 54 and 55 |
| ☐ use adjectives before nouns. | 55 |
| ☐ ask and answer questions about time. | 56 and 57 |
| ☐ make suggestions with *Let's*. | 57 |
| ☐ name at least 6 adjectives to describe places. | 54 and 55 |
| ☐ name at least 10 words for neighborhood places. | 54 and 55 |
| ☐ give times for events. | 56 and 57 |
| ☐ answer *Me too* or *Me neither* to show I'm like someone. | 58 and 59 |
| ☐ answer *Right* or *I know* to agree. | 59 |
| ☐ use prepositions *at*, *from*, *in*, *on*, and *to* with times, places, and days. | 61 |

*(Row labels at left: Grammar, Vocabulary, Conversation strategies, Writing)*

## Illustration credits

**Ken Batelman:** 42   **Harry Briggs:** 15, 61 *(4 at bottom)*, 69   **Domninic Bugatto:** 8, 23, 27, 38, 59, 78   **Cambridge University Press:** 67
**Matt Collins:** 22, 54   **Chuck Gonzales:** 5, 11, 26, 45, 80   **Cheryl Hoffman:** 3, 24, 47, 61 *(2 at top)*   **Jon Keegan:** 19, 51, 94, 95
**Frank Montagna:** 2, 13, 21, 53, 82, 83   **Greg White:** 7, 16, 37, 79   **Terry Wong:** 30, 46, 63, 74, 86   **Filip Yip:** 70

## Photo credits

**3** *(clockwise from top left)* ©Exactostock/SuperStock; ©Elea Dumas/Getty Images; ©MIXA/Getty Images; ©Thinkstock   **4** ©Ryan McVay/Getty Images   **7** ©wavebreakmedia/Shutterstock   **10** *(clockwise from top left)* ©Andresr/Shutterstock; ©MTPA Stock/Masterfile; ©Spencer Grant/PhotoEdit; ©Jose Luiz Pelaez Inc./Corbis; ©Medioimages/Photodisc/Thinkstock; ©Terry Doyle/Getty Images   **11** *(top to bottom)* ©Image Source/SuperStock; ©kurhan/Shutterstock   **12** *(pen)* ©Phant/Shutterstock; *(potato chips)* ©Thinkstock; *(wallet)* ©AlexTois/Shutterstock; *(laptop)* ©Alex Staroseltsev/Shutterstock; *(umbrella)* ©K. Miri Photography/Shutterstock; *(bag)* ©Hemera Technologies/Thinkstock; *(glasses)* ©Ingvar Bjork/Shutterstock; *(keys)* ©SELEZNEV VALERY/Shutterstock; *(notebook)* ©zirconicusso/Shutterstock; *(smartphone)* ©Oleksiy Mark/Shutterstock; *(water bottle)* ©lucadp/Shutterstock; *(eraser)* ©GreenStockCreative/Shutterstock; *(watch)* ©Venus Angel/Shutterstock; ©Butterfly Hunter/Shutterstock; *(pencil)* ©Julia Ivantsova/Shutterstock; *(hand holding smartphone)* ©Thinkstock; *(hand holding water bottle)* ©DenisNata/Shutterstock; *(all others)* ©George Kerrigan   **14** *(top row, left to right)* ©Rtimages/Shutterstock; ©Cambridge University Press; ©Thinkstock; ©Cambridge University Press *(middle row, left to right)* ©Ryan McVay/Thinkstock; ©Ryan McVay/Thinkstock; ©Thinkstock; ©Pixtal/age Fotostock *(bottom row, left to right)* ©Cambridge University Press; ©Cambridge University Press; ©Photodisc/Thinkstock; ©vovan/Shutterstock   **19** ©Design Pics/SuperStock   **20** *(clockwise from top left)* ©Exactostock/SuperStock; ©Exactostock/SuperStock; ©Mark Scott/Getty Images; ©Fancy Collection/SuperStock; ©Andreas Pollok/Getty Images; ©Ron Chapple/Getty Images; ©rSnapshotPhotos/Shutterstock; ©Peter Cade/Getty Images   **28** ©Don Nichols/Getty Images   **29** *(top to bottom)* ©Larry Dale Gordon/Getty Image; ©Punchstock   **32** *(television)* ©Maxx-Studio/Shutterstock   **35** *(top to bottom)* ©Darren Mower/Getty Images; ©Thinkstock   **36** *(top row, left to right)* ©JOSE LUIS SALMERON Notimex/Newscom; ©The Everett Collection; ©The Everett Collection; ©Getty Images *(bottom row, left to right)* ©Lions Gate/courtesy Everett Collection; ©Eric Roberts/Corbis; ©Robert Voets/CBS via Getty Images; ©Ann Johansson/Corbis   **40** ©violetblue/Shutterstock   **43** *(left to right)* ©Maxx-Studio/Shutterstock; ©MariusdeGraf/Shutterstock   **44** *(clockwise from top left)* ©Cambridge University Press; ©Artur Synenko/Shutterstock; ©Cambridge University Press; ©Cambridge University Press; ©Cambridge University Press; ©Cambridge University Press   **45** ©Punchstock   **47** ©Anders Blomqvist/Getty Images   **48** *(left to right)* ©Ambient Images Inc./Alamy; ©Yellow Dog Productions/Getty Images; ©Spencer Grant/PhotoEdit; ©David Grossman/Imageworks   **50** *(clockwise from top left)* ©Holly Harris/Getty Images; © Kwame Zikomo/SuperStock; © Jens Lucking/Getty Image; © Kaz Chiba/Getty Images; © Onoky/SuperStock; © I. Hatz/Masterfile   **52** *(top row, all photos)* ©Cambridge University Press *(middle row, left to right)* ©Cambridge University Press; ©Rudy Umans/Shutterstock; ©JupiterImages *(bottom row, left to right)* ©JupiterImages; ©Cambridge University Press; ©Danilo Calilung/Corbis   **56** ©Mike Powell/Getty Images   **58** *(sweater)* ©Karina Bakalyan/Shutterstock; *(skirt)* ©Ruslan Kudrin/Shutterstock; *(jeans)* ©Karkas/Shutterstock *(all others)* ©Cambridge University Press   **60** ©George Kerrigan   **64** *(clockwise from top left)* ©Belinda Images/SuperStock; ©Ingram Publishing/SuperStock; ©Blend Images/SuperStock; ©Punchstock *(mouse)* ©urfin/Shutterstock   **66** *(top row, left to right)* ©Catherine Karnow/Corbis; ©Shawn Baldwin/EPA/Newscom; ©Fotosonline/Alamy *(middle row, left to right)* ©Peter Willi/SuperStock; ©Douglas Pulsipher/Alamy; ©KSTFoto/Alamy (bottom row, left to right) ©Cambridge University Press; ©Prisma Bildagentur AG/Alamy; ©S.T. Yiap Still Life/Alamy   **67** *(top to bottom)* ©Bob Krist/Corbis; ©Ron Erwin/Getty Images; ©Bert Hoferichter/Alamy   **68** *(clockwise from top left)* ©Enzo/agefotostock; ©Olga Lyubkina/Shutterstock; ©Olga Miltsova/Shutterstock; ©Joseph Dilag/Shutterstock   **69** ©Steve Hix/Somos Images/Corbis   **71** *(top to bottom)* ©Laura Coles/Getty Images; ©Datacraft Co Ltd/Getty Images; ©panda3800/Shutterstock   **72** *(top to bottom)* ©Stephen Johnson/Getty Images; ©Simon DesRochers/Masterfile; ©ImagesEurope/Alamy; ©David Robinson/Snap2000 Images/Alamy75 © Best View Stock/Alamy   **76** ©Thinkstock   **82** ©Thinkstock   **84** *(top to bottom)* ©Exactostock/SuperStock; ©Joe McBride/Getty Images   **85** ©David Young-Wolff/PhotoEdit   **87** ©Blend Images/SuperStock   **90** *(clockwise from top left)* ©Cambridge University Press; ©Alexander Raths/Shutterstock; ©Cambridge University Press; ©Africa Studio/Shutterstock; ©Cambridge University Press; ©Cambridge University Press; ©Cambridge University Press; ©Cambridge University Press; ©Lepas/Shutterstock; ©Luis Carlos Jimenez del rio/Shutterstock; ©Jonelle Weaver/Getty Images; ©Cambridge University Press; ©Tetra Images/SuperStock; ©Cambridge University Press; ©Nixx Photography/Shutterstock; ©Orange Stock Photo Production Inc./Alamy; ©simpleman/Shutterstock   **91** ©jet/Shutterstock   **92** (top row, left to right) ©Cambridge University Press; ©Cambridge University Press; ©Cambridge University Press; ©Thinkstock; ©Cambridge University Press *(top middle row, left to right)* ©Ryan McVay/Thinkstock; ©Valentyn Volkov/Shutterstock; ©Thinkstock; ©Cambridge University Press; ©Cambridge University Press *(bottom middle row, left to right)* ©Cambridge University Press; ©Cambridge University Press; ©Cambridge University Press; ©Cambridge University Press; ©Multiart/Shutterstock (bottom row, left to right) ©Cambridge University Press; ©Cambridge University Press; ©Cambridge University Press; ©Cambridge University Press; ©svry/Shutterstock   **93** *(top to bottom)* ©Cambridge University Press; ©Thinkstock; ©Thinkstock; ©Fuse/Getty Images/RF   **96** ©Lena Pantiukh/Shutterstock

## Text credits

While every effort has been made, it has not always been possible to identify the sources of all the material used, or to trace all copyright holders. If any omissions are brought to our notice, we will be happy to include the appropriate acknowledgements on reprinting.

Special thanks to Kerry S. Vrabel for his editorial contributions.

# The top 500 spoken words

This is a list of the top 500 words in spoken North American English. It is based on a sample of four and a half million words of conversation from the Cambridge International Corpus. The most frequent word, *I*, is at the top of the list.

| | | |
|---|---|---|
| 1. I | 40. really | 79. see |
| 2. and | 41. with | 80. how |
| 3. the | 42. he | 81. they're |
| 4. you | 43. one | 82. kind |
| 5. uh | 44. are | 83. here |
| 6. to | 45. this | 84. from |
| 7. a | 46. there | 85. did |
| 8. that | 47. I'm | 86. something |
| 9. it | 48. all | 87. too |
| 10. of | 49. if | 88. more |
| 11. yeah | 50. no | 89. very |
| 12. know | 51. get | 90. want |
| 13. in | 52. about | 91. little |
| 14. like | 53. at | 92. been |
| 15. they | 54. out | 93. things |
| 16. have | 55. had | 94. an |
| 17. so | 56. then | 95. you're |
| 18. was | 57. because | 96. said |
| 19. but | 58. go | 97. there's |
| 20. is | 59. up | 98. I've |
| 21. it's | 60. she | 99. much |
| 22. we | 61. when | 100. where |
| 23. huh | 62. them | 101. two |
| 24. just | 63. can | 102. thing |
| 25. oh | 64. would | 103. her |
| 26. do | 65. as | 104. didn't |
| 27. don't | 66. me | 105. other |
| 28. that's | 67. mean | 106. say |
| 29. well | 68. some | 107. back |
| 30. for | 69. good | 108. could |
| 31. what | 70. got | 109. their |
| 32. on | 71. OK | 110. our |
| 33. think | 72. people | 111. guess |
| 34. right | 73. now | 112. yes |
| 35. not | 74. going | 113. way |
| 36. um | 75. were | 114. has |
| 37. or | 76. lot | 115. down |
| 38. my | 77. your | 116. we're |
| 39. be | 78. time | 117. any |

# The top 500 spoken words

| | | |
|---|---|---|
| 118. he's | 161. five | 204. sort |
| 119. work | 162. always | 205. great |
| 120. take | 163. school | 206. bad |
| 121. even | 164. look | 207. we've |
| 122. those | 165. still | 208. another |
| 123. over | 166. around | 209. car |
| 124. probably | 167. anything | 210. true |
| 125. him | 168. kids | 211. whole |
| 126. who | 169. first | 212. whatever |
| 127. put | 170. does | 213. twenty |
| 128. years | 171. need | 214. after |
| 129. sure | 172. us | 215. ever |
| 130. can't | 173. should | 216. find |
| 131. pretty | 174. talking | 217. care |
| 132. gonna | 175. last | 218. better |
| 133. stuff | 176. thought | 219. hard |
| 134. come | 177. doesn't | 220. haven't |
| 135. these | 178. different | 221. trying |
| 136. by | 179. money | 222. give |
| 137. into | 180. long | 223. I'd |
| 138. went | 181. used | 224. problem |
| 139. make | 182. getting | 225. else |
| 140. than | 183. same | 226. remember |
| 141. year | 184. four | 227. might |
| 142. three | 185. every | 228. again |
| 143. which | 186. new | 229. pay |
| 144. home | 187. everything | 230. try |
| 145. will | 188. many | 231. place |
| 146. nice | 189. before | 232. part |
| 147. never | 190. though | 233. let |
| 148. only | 191. most | 234. keep |
| 149. his | 192. tell | 235. children |
| 150. doing | 193. being | 236. anyway |
| 151. cause | 194. bit | 237. came |
| 152. off | 195. house | 238. six |
| 153. I'll | 196. also | 239. family |
| 154. maybe | 197. use | 240. wasn't |
| 155. real | 198. through | 241. talk |
| 156. why | 199. feel | 242. made |
| 157. big | 200. course | 243. hundred |
| 158. actually | 201. what's | 244. night |
| 159. she's | 202. old | 245. call |
| 160. day | 203. done | 246. saying |

# The top 500 spoken words

| | | |
|---|---|---|
| 247. dollars | 290. started | 333. believe |
| 248. live | 291. job | 334. thinking |
| 249. away | 292. says | 335. funny |
| 250. either | 293. play | 336. state |
| 251. read | 294. usually | 337. until |
| 252. having | 295. wow | 338. husband |
| 253. far | 296. exactly | 339. idea |
| 254. watch | 297. took | 340. name |
| 255. week | 298. few | 341. seven |
| 256. mhm | 299. child | 342. together |
| 257. quite | 300. thirty | 343. each |
| 258. enough | 301. buy | 344. hear |
| 259. next | 302. person | 345. help |
| 260. couple | 303. working | 346. nothing |
| 261. own | 304. half | 347. parents |
| 262. wouldn't | 305. looking | 348. room |
| 263. ten | 306. someone | 349. today |
| 264. interesting | 307. coming | 350. makes |
| 265. am | 308. eight | 351. stay |
| 266. sometimes | 309. love | 352. mom |
| 267. bye | 310. everybody | 353. sounds |
| 268. seems | 311. able | 354. change |
| 269. heard | 312. we'll | 355. understand |
| 270. goes | 313. life | 356. such |
| 271. called | 314. may | 357. gone |
| 272. point | 315. both | 358. system |
| 273. ago | 316. type | 359. comes |
| 274. while | 317. end | 360. thank |
| 275. fact | 318. least | 361. show |
| 276. once | 319. told | 362. thousand |
| 277. seen | 320. saw | 363. left |
| 278. wanted | 321. college | 364. friends |
| 279. isn't | 322. ones | 365. class |
| 280. start | 323. almost | 366. already |
| 281. high | 324. since | 367. eat |
| 282. somebody | 325. days | 368. small |
| 283. let's | 326. couldn't | 369. boy |
| 284. times | 327. gets | 370. paper |
| 285. guy | 328. guys | 371. world |
| 286. area | 329. god | 372. best |
| 287. fun | 330. country | 373. water |
| 288. they've | 331. wait | 374. myself |
| 289. you've | 332. yet | 375. run |

# The top 500 spoken words

| | | |
|---|---|---|
| 376. they'll | 418. company | 460. sorry |
| 377. won't | 419. friend | 461. living |
| 378. movie | 420. set | 462. drive |
| 379. cool | 421. minutes | 463. outside |
| 380. news | 422. morning | 464. bring |
| 381. number | 423. between | 465. easy |
| 382. man | 424. music | 466. stop |
| 383. basically | 425. close | 467. percent |
| 384. nine | 426. leave | 468. hand |
| 385. enjoy | 427. wife | 469. gosh |
| 386. bought | 428. knew | 470. top |
| 387. whether | 429. pick | 471. cut |
| 388. especially | 430. important | 472. computer |
| 389. taking | 431. ask | 473. tried |
| 390. sit | 432. hour | 474. gotten |
| 391. book | 433. deal | 475. mind |
| 392. fifty | 434. mine | 476. business |
| 393. months | 435. reason | 477. anybody |
| 394. women | 436. credit | 478. takes |
| 395. month | 437. dog | 479. aren't |
| 396. found | 438. group | 480. question |
| 397. side | 439. turn | 481. rather |
| 398. food | 440. making | 482. twelve |
| 399. looks | 441. American | 483. phone |
| 400. summer | 442. weeks | 484. program |
| 401. hmm | 443. certain | 485. without |
| 402. fine | 444. less | 486. moved |
| 403. hey | 445. must | 487. gave |
| 404. student | 446. dad | 488. yep |
| 405. agree | 447. during | 489. case |
| 406. mother | 448. lived | 490. looked |
| 407. problems | 449. forty | 491. certainly |
| 408. city | 450. air | 492. talked |
| 409. second | 451. government | 493. beautiful |
| 410. definitely | 452. eighty | 494. card |
| 411. spend | 453. wonderful | 495. walk |
| 412. happened | 454. seem | 496. married |
| 413. hours | 455. wrong | 497. anymore |
| 414. war | 456. young | 498. you'll |
| 415. matter | 457. places | 499. middle |
| 416. supposed | 458. girl | 500. tax |
| 417. worked | 459. happen | |